# THINGS THAT MAKE ME FEEL BETTER

A collection of words from the heart & mind

By: Bri Car

For the 18 year old me,
who wrote half of these pieces...
Thanks for being such an angsty
teen.

And, for the person reading
this... Without you, there would
be no need to share.

Thank you.

I guess we could also add my
dog, Captain.
Cap, you're a little shit,
and I love you.

# THE BREAKUP

## THINGS THAT MAKE ME FEEL BETTER

I hate how many things make me think of you.

I'm sitting in a coffee shop, & a song you once showed me comes on.

Before I know it, without even trying, you're back in my head, taking up residency. I want nothing more than to burn the memory of you from my mind, to evict you from your never-ending home in my head.

I want you gone.

And yet, you're everywhere.

THINGS THAT MAKE ME FEEL BETTER

I feel my insides pushing out.
I think I may throw up.
I can't believe what's happening.
I'm not some runner-up.

I'm sure I won't forget you
for you left a massive mark.
But deep inside, I'm crumbling.
There's no longer a spark.

I like to think you miss me,
though it may be empty hope.
But either way, it's helping me
to move on and to cope.

Your face still haunts me nightly.
I can hear you in my sleep.
And though it pains me to admit,
sometimes I even weep.

I know I shouldn't miss you
since you weren't mine to begin.
But somehow I still find myself
Wishing we'd never end.

I know it's partly my fault;
It's a choice I still regret.
But honestly, I never thought
you'd be hard to forget.

THINGS THAT MAKE ME FEEL BETTER

Your face is ugly
& you're stupid
& your forehead is too big
& you'll be bald by 30.

BYE.

He told me that he loved me,
but I knew it was a lie.
He likes to tell me anything
to make sure I don't cry.

Like that time we went to Boston,
and his driver made him late,
and I acted like I didn't know
that he was on a date.

I could smell her musky perfume.
Feel the sweat drip down his back.
A clueless side chick, I assume.
I'm shocked I didn't hack.

I took the break-up modestly.
In fact, I'm quite surprised.
He found his shit across the yard –
and this time, HE'S who cried.

You came out of nowhere.
You caught me off guard.
We just started talking
like it wasn't hard.

I couldn't believe it
when you said hello
since our last goodbye
seemed so long ago.

We just made some small talk
about work and friends.
My head kept on thinking
"Oh when will this end?".

You finally came in
for that awkward hug,
and just as you showed up,
you flew like a bug.

I can't believe I let you leave.
Oh how time slips away.
And even when you had to go,
I wished that you could stay.

Now all that's left are memories
I think about each day.
I'm slowly drowning in the pain
of words I couldn't say.

### THINGS THAT MAKE ME FEEL BETTER

You'd think I'd be used
to my heart getting crushed.
Repeatedly stabbed,
down a toilet it's flushed.

I thought you'd be different,
but now I can see.
You're just like the rest,
and it's killing me.

Don't take me too seriously,
not that you would,
but think what went wrong
once I'm all gone for good.

He looks her in the eyes.
She trips & falls again.
He doesn't even care
that he's messing with her head.

And so the story goes.
It drives her so insane.
And yet, she lets him mess around,
and play her like a game.

## THINGS THAT MAKE ME FEEL BETTER

You tell me that you love me,
and you swear you mean it now.
This isn't like the last time,
but I'm still wondering how.

Cause every time she calls you
just to see what's going on,
conveniently I'm not around;
I feel like such a pawn.

She'll ask you out to dinner,
Or to come see her new place.
You say that you're just friends,
But I see it on your face.

You tell me that you love me,
But I think it's time you hear:
I'm sick of all your bullshit,
And your love is no good here.

# THE EXISTENCE

# THINGS THAT MAKE ME FEEL BETTER

Take the **FUCKING** chance.

## THINGS THAT MAKE ME FEEL BETTER

She's a beautiful mix
of wonder & bliss
with hands in her pockets
and sin on her lips.

BRI CAR

Sometimes I have to step back,
and think about what makes me happy.
And usually around that time,
I realize the answer's

me.

THINGS THAT MAKE ME FEEL BETTER

I'm so proud of you.

You're working your tail off
and chasing dreams
and not letting anyone stop you.

Keep reaching past what people think
possible.
Keep believing in yourself.
Keep running toward your well deserved
happy ending.

It will come.

I used to listen closely.
When they'd talk, I'd hear them out.
I used to think the things they said
would help me build some clout.

I cared about opinions.
They stuck on me like tattoos.
I compromised my favorite things,
and made myself feel blue.

I knew it didn't matter,
but for some reason, to me
I felt I needed to impress
to prove who I could be.

It really is so silly.
You would think by now I'd know
that keeping up with everyone
is really just a show.

I'm not too great an actress.
If I were, I'd be a star.
But honestly, it's all too much;
It leaves too many scars.

THINGS THAT MAKE ME FEEL BETTER

Oh, I'm sorry...

Did my confidence scare you??

Good.

You ask me how I'm doing,
and I tend to say "just fine",
but deep inside's a monster,
and he's trapping me in vines.

They wrap around my neck,
so at times I cannot speak.
They paralyze my body
to the point where I feel weak.

I'm trying to get better.
Every day's a battle won.
With every breath that steadies me,
I pray the monster's done.

THINGS THAT MAKE ME FEEL BETTER

Don't you dare
let them tell you who they think

# YOU

are.

I'm trying to talk,
but you won't even listen.
I'm trying to show you
my dreams and my vision.

I know you don't get it.
It's easy to see.
But why can't you just try
to have faith in me?

I can't even tell you
the thoughts in my head
for fear that I just might
be chained to my bed.

I'm trying to branch out
and do something new,
and if you support me,
I'll prove it to you.

## THINGS THAT MAKE ME FEEL BETTER

What do you do
when the best part of you
gets trampled
and stomped on
and turns black & blue?

When you can't move a muscle,
and you can't find a smile,
turn your back on the world;
take a break for a while.

When did we become so dependent
on everything around us
instead of looking into our hearts
for the answers to everything
that swirls around in our heads?

## THINGS THAT MAKE ME FEEL BETTER

My worth is not dependent
on the boobs across my chest.
You cannot base my money
on my kitten heels and dress.

You cannot interrupt me
just because you have a thought.
I know this might sound crazy,
but my silence can't be bought.

I do not march for exercise
as per your last request.
And when my kid gets hungry,
you might have to see my breast.

Life or death is easy
when the body isn't yours.
And after work, you best believe,
you're helping with the chores.

The theory that we all hate men
is really just made up.
But if you try to cross the line,
I'll tell you this: Time's Up.

# THE LOVE

## THINGS THAT MAKE ME FEEL BETTER

Something in me says he's the one.

That one day, maybe down the road,
              we'll meet again,
        and we'll touch again,
and we'll be mad for each other,

        until death do us part.

THINGS THAT MAKE ME FEEL BETTER

Her black, heartless soul
gets lighter each day.
Before the devil can scold,
angel's push him away.

Dogs were placed on this Earth
so that we'd have someone

to talk to
and cry to
and laugh to

without ever being judged.

That
is the definition of true love.

THINGS THAT MAKE ME FEEL BETTER

Her mind's saying no,
while her body says yes.
She knows that she'll lose,
but which way is a guess.

The way that she was giggling,
and the smile on his face
made me realize in that moment
that their love was sent from grace.

There was something truly special
in the way they said "I do".
And the kiss that shortly followed
was so passionate and true.

She had found her ever after.
There was no doubt in my mind
that the two of them would flourish
happily through all of time.

## THINGS THAT MAKE ME FEEL BETTER

I can't put into words
what I'm feeling for you now.
I don't know when it happened,
and I'm still not quite sure how.

I don't know if it's dangerous,
or even worth the fight.
But you're the last thing on my mind
before I sleep at night.

Your name pops up on my cell phone
and all the world stops.
I feel my heartbeat start to race
like I got caught by cops.

I don't know if you realize
that inside you're killing me.
But every time I think of you,
I think of what could be.

## THINGS THAT MAKE ME FEEL BETTER

Please remember
forever and always
that only
you
can make yourself truly happy.

Not money
Not another person
Not a city
Not a pet

You are responsible for the joy
that surrounds you.

In loving yourself, you are loving
the world.

I don't understand where we're going,
but I'm tired of tagging along.

If I'm on your mind,
then stop wasting time.
I've been waiting on you for so long.

THINGS THAT MAKE ME FEEL BETTER

heartbreak
and
passion
and
butterflies

mean nothing
compared to the love
I have for
you.

Thank you for your
time
and
support
and
compassion.

Forever
&
Always

xoxo Bri

Made in the USA
Lexington, KY
02 February 2019